Essay: I FAILED, I wrote a Book and it didn't sell
Copyright © 2016 by Kevin Caster

Requests for information should be addressed to:
Gate Beautiful, LLC
christiandave@cfl.rr.com

I0442023

ISBN-13 978-1523216239
ISBN-10 1523216239

Editors Note:
I'm not a great writer. I'm not great at grammar.
This effort is not professionally edited and to be
honest wasn't even proof read that much. This
was written more or less as a stream of
conscience. If this actually sells enough copies
then maybe I'll put up the money to get it edited.

Purpose:
Please do better than me. I want to share my
story. I clearly don't have all the answers
because my book didn't sell so you may read
this and say "oh what a bonehead he clearly
should have done x, y, and z different". I'm not
sure that I would change anything but having
my experience mapped out before you may help
you have a better result.

Important Info:
As I researched the Internet on book sales, I
observed that the odds were against me. The
average book sells 20 copies. Presumably those
are just to family and friends. I'm one of the
statistics, one of the hardest things I found to do
was to get a random stranger to buy my book.

Predatory?:

Again as I researched the publishing process on the Internet, I felt it was somewhat predatory in particular for children's books which is what I wanted to write. I found many companies that offered the service to edit, illustrate, publish, and advertise my book. The barrier to entry to write a children's book is really low. It doesn't require amazing prose, a detailed story with great character development and a twist, or hundreds and hundreds of hours of research and typing. Because the barrier is so low there are many people inspired to try and give it a shot. So much so there is an entire industry to support authors that want to create a children's book. That's the part that made me feel this segment could be predatory. If the average book sells 20 copies how could it make sense to spend $15K-$20K to write one? I didn't go with the one stop shop option so maybe I'm off base. It was just the feeling I got.

In the beginning:
Several years ago I had an inkling of an idea for a children's book. My kids were little at the time and I read a ton of children's books. In my opinion most of them were just okay. I thought to myself, "I can take a stab at this". I honestly thought I could produce something that was at or above the quality of what we had bought. At the time I was a late 30's professional that creates and solves problems for a living. How hard could this be?

Research:
The first effort was to try and figure out all the steps required to take a book from the idea of wanting to do something to taking it to market. I wanted to understand the whole path. I also wanted to know what the cost would likely be.

Idea:

For my book, I wanted to try and come up with a unique idea. I looked on Kick Starter to see what kind of books regular Joe's like me were doing. I also looked on some self publishing websites. In seem like most of the story lines for those books were me-too's of what was out there. There wasn't anything unique or compelling. From what I could tell there were a bunch of books about the family pet. We have a cat that is really cool, and it crossed my mind to make him the subject of the book. After seeing all these books about family pets I realized I could care less about their pet so why would anyone care about mine? Certainly no one would care enough to pay money to read a story about my cat. There are some famous examples of where this did work, but I felt like this path was a me too and likely to fail.

I also looked at major big box stores and saw what they were selling. For the most part they sold licensed children's books. I also observed famous people writing children's books. In the big box store it all seemed about giving the consumer a reason to care about the book.

I continued to do research on ideas. I wrote down a bunch. I then did an Internet search on them. I pulled up the images link. I looked for an image that might strike a feeling that might be compelling. I like faith based books and one of the ideas I had was a book on prayer. I found an image of a boy praying in a classroom. The image was moving. It had stood the test of time. It was taken in 1966 and was used as a B photo for an article on the same subject. I actually tracked down the image owner and got permission to include the image in my book. The image was so compelling I thought if I have any chance to break through the noise it was to use this image as my inspiration. That image was already pre-selected several times, it had been published in a newspaper, had made it to a photo archive, was used for a recent article, and had stopped me in my tracks.

At this point I honestly let myself believe that I had a decent chance of beating the odds and creating something that could sell a 1000 copies. A book on prayer at school seemed compelling. How great would it be to have a tool to talk to our children about how important it is to pray outside of church and outside of the home. Public prayer makes many uncomfortable. Even at Christmas dinner this past year our host found it difficult to find someone willing to step up and bless the dinner. I convinced myself if I had a good idea. I convinced myself that if I saw this book in the store, like at the checkout counter, I would be compelled to pick it up.

As a creator of something I didn't prepare myself for what if it doesn't resonate, what if no one likes it. There are far more pictures taken, drawn, and painted than ever get purchased. The same goes with books and music. I've come to realize it is extremely difficult to create something that anyone will ever buy. Maybe it is better not to know the odds. If everyone thought the challenge was too hard nobody would ever try. It's kind of like the adage you can't win the lottery if you don't buy a ticket. Similarly you can't become a best selling author if you don't write a book.

Book Outline:
I started by pulling out my daughter's book collection and reading. I read the pages with an intent of figuring out how to tell a story that would match how a children's book is written. I felt learning from professionals was the best way to go.
I sketched up an outline and wrote out the dialog for a couple of key pages.

Illustrator and Type Setter
I then went to LinkedIn and looked under Children Book Illustrators and I reached out to several and asked them for a quote. I shared with them a brief summary of the book with some key text and the page count. The illustrators were all generous to answer my questions and provide quotes for estimation purposes.

What I quickly realized is that some illustrators are just illustrators and some do both type setting and illustrating. Initially I didn't understand the difference but the Type Setter is the one that chooses the font and the placement of the text over the picture. I'm not sure how this wouldn't have to be the same person. If it wasn't then there would have to be a ton of interaction between the Illustrator and the Type Setter. I decided that I wanted someone that could do both the type setting and the illustrating.

All the illustrators I looked at had examples of their work on the Internet. I looked through their example artwork to find the best fit. I found the one that was perfect for me. She could do both illustration and type setting. She had experience, she even had a book she illustrated that had sold 25,000 copies. I loved her work and her quote was reasonable. I won't give the exact amount because I'm sure it depends on many factors but the quotes I got back ranged from $5K to $15K. I'm not sure if all the contracts are the same way but for the one I went with, the illustration gets half of the profit after the author makes back all their money. That's why I felt it was important to make sure I sold the illustrator on book idea. That would likely factor into whether or not she would take on the project and how much she might charge.

I did think I could do it cheaper if I got an art student at the local high school or someone at church that was a hobbyist. But I decided that my best bet was to use a professional. I thought if I had someone involved with the project that had been successful previously my odds of success would greatly improve.

First Development Tools:
I had no idea what development tools I should use so I started out with what turned out to be the hard way. I have a MAC and was drawn to the iBooks Author because it was advertised as a tool to both develop the book as well as a method to publish the book on iBooks. So that's what I started with.

Number of pages:
After some research I determined that most children's books are 32 interior pages. For mass production the number of pages has to be divisible by 8. This seems to make sense when you think about the construction of the book. The 32 interior pages basically include a single page in the front, 15 double pages, and a single page at the end. So when writing the story it's important that it fit within this framework. It is possible to do a book that is 24 pages and it also is possible to have some blank pages at the end.

Manuscript:
I originally wrote the book using a word processing tool. This was helpful as it does basic spell checking and grammar checks. It's also easy to cut and paste and move things around. I wanted to make sure I had made the best use of the hard page count.

Editor:

I decided that I needed an editor. I felt that I had read the copy a million times and might have overlooked something. Also as you can see from this effort my grammar isn't perfect. Again I felt like if I wanted a chance to sell a 1000 copies having it professionally edited would be well worth it. Besides just checking for grammar and spelling the editor also game me feedback on writing style and the story line. Again just for estimation purposes I received quotes from $50 to $200 to edit the book. It was worth every penny. The editor I worked was really great. He gave me some great notes and made my project come across really professional.

If I were to do it again and cost were no object, I would probably change a couple things. First I might consider a ghost writer. Let's face it a professional writer will have a way with words and will have a better feel for how to construct the story. In my daughter's book collection there were some phrases that I couldn't replicate the beauty and simplicity with which they were written. For a children's book this probably isn't critical but is an area that I could have improved.

I also realize that I should have used less words. What I wrote in my book was probably too complicated. I had a so much I wanted to say. I probably should have cut my word count by 50%.

It was good that I written the manuscript in a word processing tool because that's the format the editor waned. It allowed him to edit with track changes and to insert notes.

Hand off to Illustrator:
I then used iBooks author to make a crude version of the book. I staged and took pictures and searched the Internet for public domain pictures that fit the type of illustrations I wanted for that particular page. I inserted them in to the author tool and added the text, included the cover page.

This gave me a good feel for how the book would read and was a gate for me to show it off to a couple friends and family before going to the time and expense to get it illustrated.

I showed it to my daughter and she didn't know that I wrote it and she was engaged and seemed to like it and we had some good conversations about the content. I then showed it to my wife and she thought it was done well. I also showed it to someone in our church family and they thought it was good. Getting feedback is always hard. I realized that my friends and family probably aren't going to tell me that it is terrible and even if someone did tell me that it was terrible it doesn't mean that others won't like it. The only real proof is sales. Again after that feedback I convinced myself that I was happy with the product and yes it could sell a 1000 copies.

Illustration process:
iBooks author allowed me to publish the file to PDF. This was great for passing off to the illustrator/type setter. This gave her a strong basis for a quote. I believe I had to pay ¼ up front, ¼ after the sketches were approved, ¼ after half the book was complete and the final payment after the book was complete.

The illustrator did a great job. Having the example photos really helped the crude version come to life.

The biggest lesson learned, using PDF was great to aid the illustrations but was terrible for the text. She had to retype the text and that process was error prone. Eventually I asked for two versions of each page one with text and one without text. This was useful for several reasons. First I got her take on how the text should be placed and I could take the version without the text and add the text myself. This allowed me to copy directly from the professionally edited version to JPEG image. Have a version without the text also allowed me to make any last minute edits to the copy. There were a couple cases where I wanted to change some of the wording to make it more kid like.

Format:
I struggled with the size of the page. What the illustrator provided me what off of what I had asked and I didn't realize it was off until the end. I was able to rescale things to make it work but it would have been a lot easier if it was just right from the beginning.

I formatted my book so that the pages would bleed. What this means is that the illustration goes to the edge of the page. How the manufacture does this is by using oversized paper and then cutting to the final size. The manufactures require the illustration to go beyond the page. It's important that the illustrator understand this because you don't want an important image or text to be near the edge of the page because it could get cut off. This is also an issue for the interior edge in particular the center of a double page. With how the book is manufactured the center doesn't lay flat it and it's not one big page so the center area needs to not have anything important in it. I didn't realize this until it was too late. The best illustration in the book is ruined in the print version because of how the image was split. I do take solace in that it looks great in the electronic version.

I went with a manufactured book that is 6" wide x 9" tall. Submitted, a single page was 6.125"x9.250". The cover was 12.33"x9.250". The cover is put together so that the back cover is on the left and the front cover is on the right. That confused me at first but eventually made sense when I thought about that's how it would be if I printed it out. I also specified 600 pixels per inch. On the rear cover I needed to leave a space clear of text and illustration of about 3" x 2" for the bar code.

Copy Right Page
Every book needs a copy right page. I suggest looking at professionally produced books as an example. What's included in the copy right page is the ISBN number. This number is required for selling on iBooks and Amazon. I initially bought one on a website that sells ISBN numbers but I later found a way to get one for free. I'll share that shortly.

Launch:
After I finally got everything perfect I used the iBooks author to launch. It went smoothly and before long I was live on iBooks.

Economics:

I had determined long ago that I wanted to charge for the book. It's not that I wanted to make money from the book but sometime over the years I had read that people don't value things that are given to them for free. The story I remember was about a program that gave out laptops to those that couldn't afford them. The program had determined through trial and error that if they gave away the laptop to those in need they were less likely to use it and more likely to break it. They determined that if they charged $100, now this was in the day that laptops were $1000, they were more likely to use the laptop and it was less likely to break. So the take away was to sell it at a discount and not make it free. So I decided to charge 99 cents. That was the cheapest that it iBooks allowed me to charge. Out of that 99 cents, I think I would get 60 cents. So I would have to sell thousands of copies to just break even. There are famous examples of children's books that have sold millions.

My wife let her friends on Facebook know that it was for sale and just like that 1 copy was sold, to my parents. My illustrator wasn't an Apple person so she didn't even buy a copy because of the challenge of having to download iBooks onto a Windows machine.

Advertising – my first attempt:

If I was going to sell a 1000 copies I would need to advertise. I decided to join Facebook. I promptly created a Fan page for my book and started adding posts/content that I thought people would be interested in reading. I don't know that many people and it wasn't going viral so I decided that I would try and use the Facebook boost advertising. I took one of my favorite pieces of content and submitted it for a boost. Facebook allows you to target the audience so I did that. Long story short Facebook would not allow me to boost that post. They claimed that they were concerned that it was a fraudulent request. I could see their point in that I just joined, but I did provide a copy of my driver's license at their request. I also requested a second time after I had linked up with my wife and had added 10-15 friends. It did cross my mind that Facebook was concerned that what I wanted to post was either not polished enough or didn't fit the mold of what they wanted on their airwaves. That's probably not the case but either way Facebook was out as a method of advertising.

Amazon:

I then decided that I wanted to solve the limited iBooks audience issue and wanted to try and figure out how to get on Amazon. I was able to basically take the output of iBooks and got it converted to be a Kindle version on Amazon. What was interesting in this process was that I discovered that I could sign up for Amazon Select Publishing and I could advertise on Amazon. The only catch was that I had to take it down on iBooks. Since I could not figure out a way to drive traffic to iBooks and less people seems to have access to iBooks this wasn't a big sacrifice.

I got it all setup for Amazon, as a note the cheapest price they would allow me to sell it on Amazon was for $1.99 still pretty reasonable. The advertising on Amazon is pretty easy. They allow you to select search words or genre or specific products to be advertised on. The advertisement can be rather small and hard to notice so the click through rate is only about 1 of a thousand impressions. Whether or not my book got selected for the impression was dependent on an auction. When I set up the advertising campaign I had to state how much I was willing to pay for a click. If I bid more than the competition I won. The winning bid per click was somewhere between 30 cents and 50 cents. As I mentioned before it is hard to even break even on this. As you can image the click through to buy ratio is going to be low. In my first campaign, I had ~69K impressions, 71 click thrus and 1 buy. I was actually ecstatic that I had 1 buy. It meant that I had gotten 1 random person to buy the book. I was also somewhat pleased that I had got 71 people to be interested enough to click on the advertisement. As happy as I was I was also disappointed that only 1 person bought. I thought it is only $1.99, that's nothing. So I thought about how I might improve the Amazon page to try and convert some of the 71 clicks into orders.

For Kindle, Amazon allows reads to peek inside before purchasing. I actually went back into the book and moved some things around to allow the peek inside to better represent the book. I also tried improving the summary.

Advertising – my second attempt

I was sitting at a Panera I think and I overheard someone say drug companies spend as much money on developing drugs as they do on advertising them. I then thought well if I've spent $5K-10K making this book maybe I need to spend $5K - $10K to marketing it. That's what a professional would do, that's what someone that wanted to break through the average 20 copies sold barrier.

There are many companies out there offering services. I reached out to one that was specifically targeted to Amazon. I got a nice email back and an offer to talk to see what they could do for me.

I talked to someone on the phone that was not predatory at all. I explained my situation. She looked at the preview and was genuinely impressed with the illustrations. She said her company couldn't offer me a good return on my investment. Her advice was to add a hard copy version using Create Space, include an Editor's Bio, and getting some church groups to post some reviews on Amazon.

I appreciated her advice.

Create Space
I had previously looked into getting hard copies printed and it was cost prohibitive. In order to get under $10 per copy I had to buy 1000 copies, that is a $10K investment. The last thing I wanted was to buy 1000 copies and sell 20 and then have 980 copies left in my garage.

Create Space was amazing. I wish I had gone with them from the beginning. I was able to submit the book in the PDF format. They provided an ISBN for free and placed the bar code on the cover. They also placed it on Amazon along with a summary and Editor's Bio that I provided. Create Space can also generate a Kindle version. Because the Kindle version already existed, Amazon was able to link the two versions together so that when I advertised the customer had a choice between buying the Kindle version for $1.99 or the Paper version for $7.99. That's an amazing deal.

The only down side is that the preview is limited to just the front cover and the back cover – there is no peek inside.

Where do I stand now?
I did another advertising campaign on Amazon and had about half the click through rate as before and didn't have any purchases. At this point a customer is choosing to buy based upon the front cover, the back cover, the summary, Editor's Bio, and reviews. I could have the most amazing interior, the secret to happiness and they wouldn't know.

If this book has a place in this world then I need one person to take a chance on it, buy it and write a good review. Then possibly there could be a snowball affect. I also could try and reach out to church groups to post some reviews, but that's not my personality. Maybe that will be my downfall.

I try and tell myself that I may have failed but at least I tried. I try and tell myself that taking something from idea to print is a success, something few accomplish. I try and remind myself of all those artists who's work isn't worth anything until after they die – what's with that?

In the end I'm blessed to have gone through this and it is something my kids can hopefully learn from.